EXPLORING THE STATES

South Dakota

THE MOUNT RUSHMORE STATE

by Patrick Perish

BELLWETHER MEDIA • MINNEAPOLIS, MN

Note to Librarians, Teachers, and Parents:

Blastoff! Readers are carefully developed by literacy experts and combine standards-based content with developmentally appropriate text.

Level 1 provides the most support through repetition of high-frequency words, light text, predictable sentence patterns, and strong visual support.

Level 2 offers early readers a bit more challenge through varied simple sentences, increased text load, and less repetition of high-frequency words.

Level 3 advances early-fluent readers toward fluency through increased text and concept load, less reliance on visuals, longer sentences, and more literary language.

Level 4 builds reading stamina by providing more text per page, increased use of punctuation, greater variation in sentence patterns, and increasingly challenging vocabulary.

Level 5 encourages children to move from "learning to read" to "reading to learn" by providing even more text, varied writing styles, and less familiar topics.

Whichever book is right for your reader, Blastoff! Readers are the perfect books to build confidence and encourage a love of reading that will last a lifetime!

This edition first published in 2014 by Bellwether Media, Inc.

No part of this publication may be reproduced in whole or in part without written permission of the publisher. For information regarding permission, write to Bellwether Media, Inc., Attention: Permissions Department, 5357 Penn Avenue South, Minneapolis, MN 55419.

Library of Congress Cataloging-in-Publication Data

Perish, Patrick.
South Dakota / by Patrick Perish.
    pages cm. – (Blastoff! readers. Exploring the states)
Includes bibliographical references and index.
Summary: "Developed by literacy experts for students in grades three through seven, this book introduces young readers to the geography and culture of South Dakota"– Provided by publisher.
ISBN 978-1-62617-041-4 (hardcover : alk. paper)
1. South Dakota–Juvenile literature. I. Title.
F651.3.P46 2014
978.3–dc23

2013002422

Printed in the United States of America, North Mankato, MN.

Table of Contents

Where Is South Dakota?

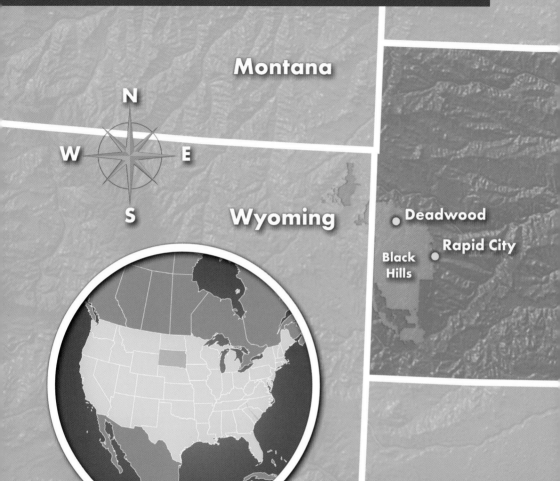

Montana

N

W   E

S

Wyoming

Deadwood

Rapid City

Black
Hills

South Dakota is located in the northern United States.
It is rectangular in shape. To the north is North Dakota.
Minnesota and Iowa are its neighbors to the east.
Nebraska shares the state's southern border. To the west
lie Wyoming and Montana.

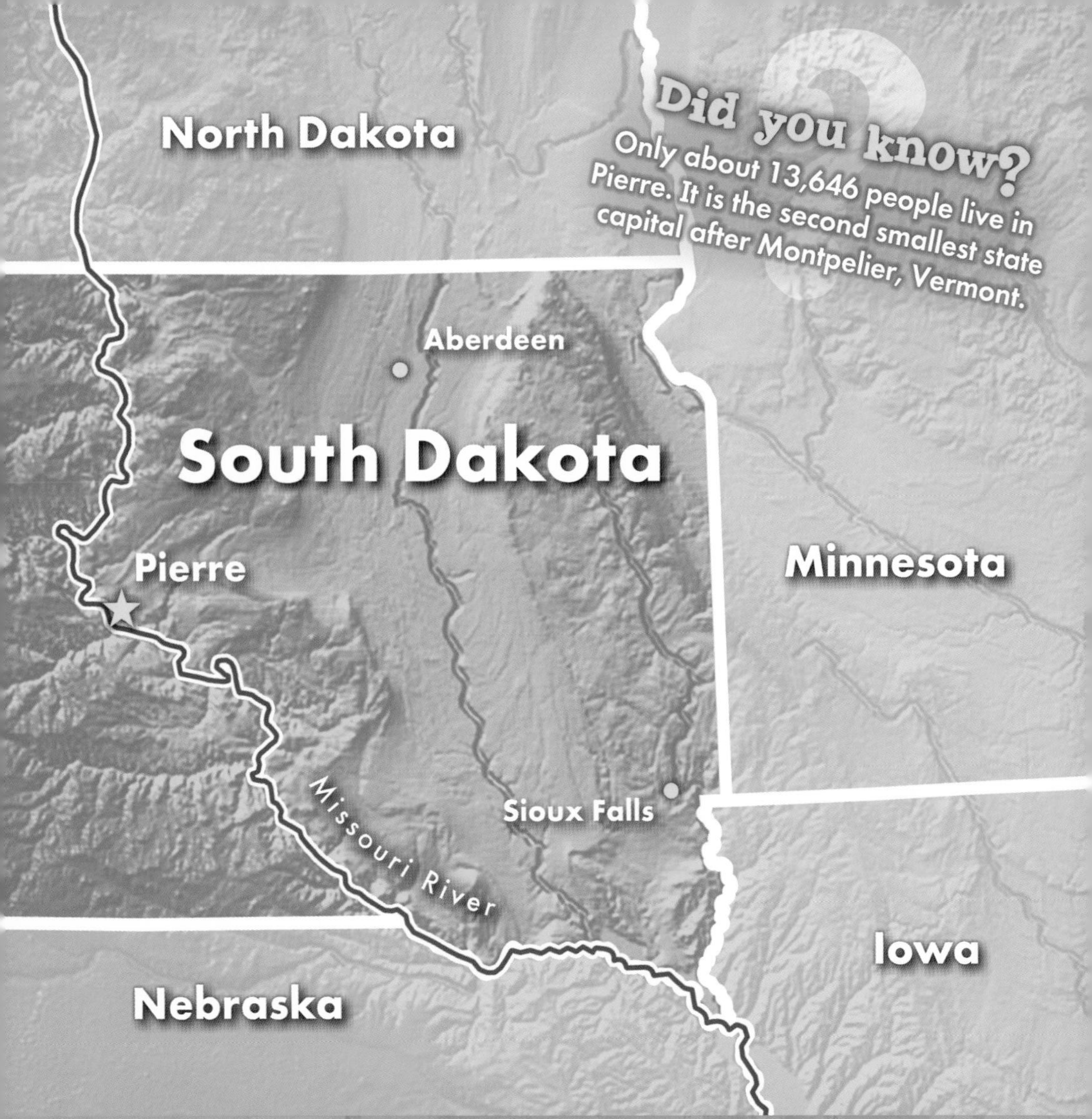

North Dakota
South Dakota
Aberdeen
Pierre
Minnesota
Sioux Falls
Missouri River
Iowa
Nebraska

Did you know?

Only about 13,646 people live in Pierre. It is the second smallest state capital after Montpelier, Vermont.

The mighty Missouri River runs down the middle of South Dakota. On its bank sits the capital, Pierre. Most South Dakotans live along the state's eastern border. Others live in the Black Hills in the west.

History

Native Americans first arrived in South Dakota around 10,000 years ago. By the 1700s, the most powerful group was the Sioux. The first Europeans came from France in the 1740s. In 1803, the French sold land that included South Dakota to the United States in the **Louisiana Purchase**. South Dakota became a state in 1889.

Sioux Native Americans

South Dakota Timeline!

1804: Meriwether Lewis and William Clark set out to explore the Louisiana Purchase territory. They follow the Missouri River through South Dakota.

1861: The Dakota Territory is formed. This includes what is now North Dakota, South Dakota, and parts of Montana and Wyoming.

1874: Gold is discovered in the Black Hills. People come from all around to strike it rich.

1876: General Custer and his army try to force the Sioux out of the Black Hills region. They are defeated in Montana in the Battle of the Little Bighorn.

1877: The U.S. government forces the Sioux to give up the Black Hills.

1889: The Dakota Territory is split. North and South Dakota become the thirty-ninth and fortieth states.

1890: The U.S. Army captures and kills more than 200 Sioux in the Wounded Knee Massacre.

1980: The U.S. Supreme Court decides that the taking of the Black Hills from the Sioux was illegal.

Battle of the Little Bighorn

Lewis and Clark

General Custer

The Land

Eastern South Dakota is defined by **prairies** and scattered lakes. The Missouri River was once known for its shifting banks and frequent flooding. It is now controlled by several **dams**. The **Great Plains** lie west of the Missouri River. These dry grasslands cover much of the state.

Between the Cheyenne and White Rivers is the strange landscape known as the Badlands. Wind and water **eroded** its beautiful valleys. Western South Dakota is home to the Black Hills. This mountainous region is heavily forested. South Dakota weather can be unpredictable. Summers are warm and sometimes very dry. Winters are cold on the plains.

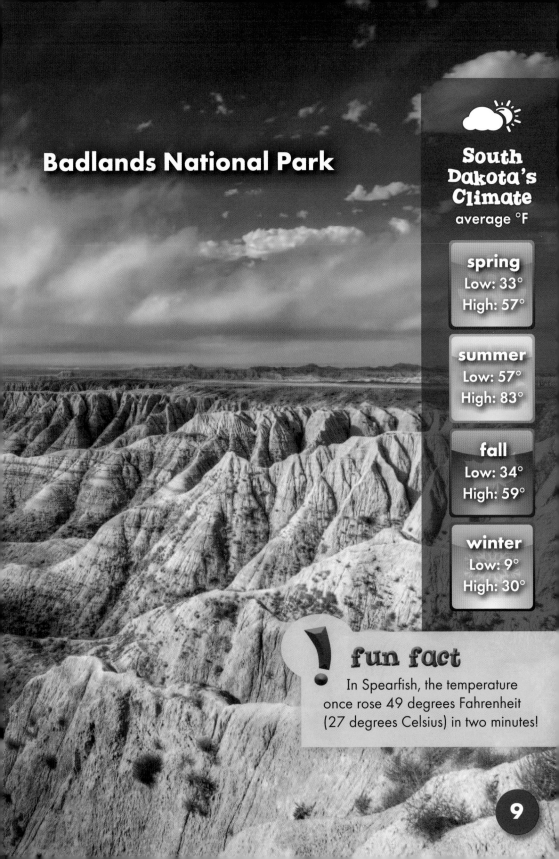

Badlands National Park

South Dakota's Climate
average °F

spring
Low: 33°
High: 57°

summer
Low: 57°
High: 83°

fall
Low: 34°
High: 59°

winter
Low: 9°
High: 30°

fun fact
In Spearfish, the temperature once rose 49 degrees Fahrenheit (27 degrees Celsius) in two minutes!

The Black Hills

Rising in South Dakota's far west are the beautiful Black Hills. Millions of years ago, pressure within the earth forced these mountains upward. Wind and water eroded them to their current size. At 7,242 feet (2,207 meters), Harney Peak is the tallest point in North America east of the Rocky Mountains. It towers over sparkling Sylvan Lake.

The Black Hills are covered in pine forests. Each year, thousands of people hike the area's tree-lined trails. Fishers and kayakers enjoy the hidden lakes and streams. The Black Hills are truly one of the nation's gems.

Harney Peak

fun fact

Thick forests make the Black Hills look dark from a distance. That is how these mountains got their name.

Wildlife

Wildlife thrives across South Dakota's many landscapes. Ducks and geese flock to the northeastern wetlands to nest. Ring-necked pheasants dart across country roads looking for cover. In the grasslands, prairie dogs, burrowing owls, and rattlesnakes make their homes underground. Above ground, pronghorns graze.

Near the Missouri River, bald eagles rest in cottonwood trees. Mountain lions prowl the rocky forests of the Black Hills. Before white settlers arrived, millions of wild bison thundered across the plains. A few small herds still survive in the national and state parks.

mountain lion

pronghorn

bald eagle

Did you know?

The pronghorn is the second fastest land animal in the world. Cheetahs are quicker, but pronghorns can run fast for longer. Pronghorns can reach top speeds of 60 miles (96.5 kilometers) per hour!

bison

fun fact !

Talk about being
big-headed! The faces of
Mount Rushmore measure
60 feet (18 meters) high.

There is a lot to see in South Dakota. In the city of Mitchell, visitors can check out the world's only Corn Palace. Each year it is decorated with more than 275,000 ears of corn. Driving west on I-90, thirsty travelers can stop at Wall Drug for its famous free ice water. Once a small town drug store, Wall Drug is now a sprawling mall and museum of the Old West.

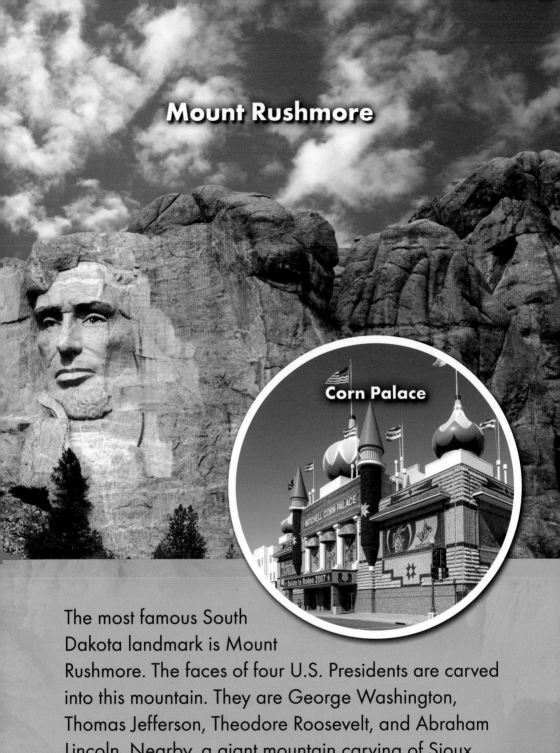

Mount Rushmore

Corn Palace

The most famous South Dakota landmark is Mount Rushmore. The faces of four U.S. Presidents are carved into this mountain. They are George Washington, Thomas Jefferson, Theodore Roosevelt, and Abraham Lincoln. Nearby, a giant mountain carving of Sioux leader Crazy Horse remains under construction.

Deadwood

The city of Deadwood was born out of the 1876 gold rush. Around 25,000 miners poured into the Black Hills looking for gold. As a **frontier** town, it was known to be a rough place. Famous **gunslinger** Wild Bill Hickok was shot over a game of cards in a Deadwood **saloon**. He is buried in the local cemetery along with Calamity Jane and other figures of the Wild West.

Visitors in Deadwood can stop at the Adams Museum to learn about the town's colorful history. At the Broken Boot Mine, people can relive the gold rush with a guided tour. In 1961, the entire town of Deadwood was named a national historic landmark.

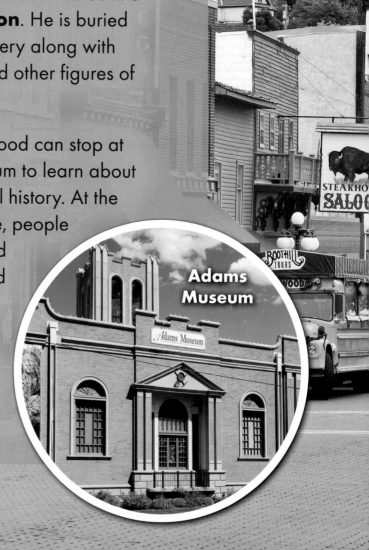

Adams Museum

Working

Farmland covers most of South Dakota. Many farmers grow hay, wheat, and corn. Others raise cattle and sheep. South Dakota is also a big honey producer. The state's factories process meat, grains, and other farm products.

The Black Hills gold rush launched the state's mining activity. Today, very little gold is mined. Instead, workers dig up granite, clay, and other useful **minerals**. Forests in the Black Hills provide lumber. Most people in South Dakota have **service jobs**. Many of them work in the shops, hotels, and restaurants in **tourist** hot spots.

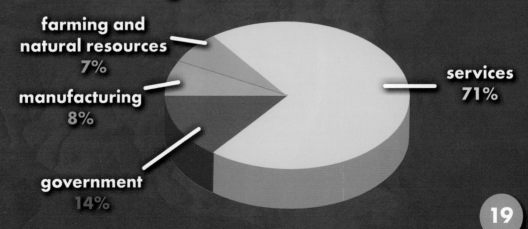

Where People Work in South Dakota

farming and natural resources 7%

manufacturing 8%

government 14%

services 71%

Playing

Many South Dakotans spend their free time outdoors. Hunters in the state bring home more than a million ring-necked pheasants each year. Fishers reel in trout from lakes and streams in the Black Hills.

The **rodeo** is South Dakota's state sport. Dozens of rodeos are held throughout the state each year. Events include barrel racing and bull riding. The Crazy Horse Volksmarch is a popular 6-mile (10-kilometer) hike in June. People can walk right up to the huge statue of Crazy Horse. This event sometimes draws more than 10,000 people.

barrel racing

Apple Cream Cheese Kuchen

Ingredients:

Crust:
1 roll sweet roll dough

Topping:
4 ounces softened cream cheese
1 tablespoon sugar
1 large tart apple, peeled and sliced
2 teaspoons butter, melted
Confectioners' sugar

Directions:

1. Thaw sweet roll dough and spread in a greased pan. Use jellyroll pan for a thinner crust or a 10x14 pan for a thicker crust.

2. In a small bowl, combine cream cheese and sugar. Spread over dough.

3. Arrange apple slices on top and brush with butter. Cover and let rise in a warm place.

4. Bake at 350°F for 25-30 minutes or until crust is golden brown and apples are tender.

5. Cool on a wire rack. Dust with confectioners' sugar. Refrigerate any leftovers.

mini fry bread tacos

pork and beans

In 2005, fry bread was named South Dakota's official bread. Native Americans first made this fried dough from government food supplies when they were forced onto **reservations**. Fry bread is popular at **powwows**. It is often served with taco fixings or honey and sugar.

Meals for early settlers included pork and beans with sides of potatoes and sourdough bread. The official state dessert is *kuchen*, or cake. German **immigrants** brought many cake recipes with them to South Dakota. A popular *kuchen* has a pie-like crust, cream cheese filling, and apple topping.

Buffalo Roundup

South Dakota has many local festivals and gatherings. The city of Clark has a yearly Potato Day celebration. One of the main events is mashed potato wrestling. The gathering also includes cook-offs and potato decorating contests.

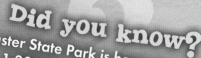

Did you know?
Custer State Park is home to around 1,300 American buffalo. Each September, cowboys and cowgirls round up the buffalo. Many people come out to see the mighty herd.

Sturgis
Motorcycle Rally

Another famous South Dakota festival is the Sturgis Motorcycle Rally. Each August, the event draws around half a million bikers to the tiny town of Sturgis. South Dakotans of all backgrounds gather to celebrate Native American culture at powwows. These festivals feature **traditional** songs and clothing. Dancing competitions are often part of the celebration.

25

The Lakota and the Black Hills

The Black Hills are **sacred** to the Lakota Sioux. The tribe calls them "the heart of everything that is." In 1868, the U.S. government signed a **treaty** that gave the Lakota the lands west of the Missouri River. Later, gold was discovered in the Black Hills. Many white people arrived hoping to get rich. The U.S. government broke its treaty and forced the Lakota out of the hills.

Today, Lakota and other South Dakotans work hard to teach people about these **injustices**. The Wounded Knee Museum has exhibits on the cruel treatment of the Sioux. Powwows give people a chance to celebrate Native American culture and keep their traditions alive. Lakota heritage is an inseparable part of South Dakota.

Oglala Lakota
Powwow

Did you know?
In 1980, the U.S. Supreme Court ruled that the taking of the Black Hills was wrong. They offered the Sioux Nation $106 million as payment, but the Sioux refused. Their sacred lands are not for sale.

Fast Facts About South Dakota

South Dakota's Flag

South Dakota's flag has a sky blue background with the state seal in the center. The seal shows a farmer across the Missouri River from a mining operation. These represent the state's major industries. Above the scene is the state motto. The seal is surrounded by sunrays and the words, "South Dakota, The Mount Rushmore State."

State Flower
American pasque

State Nicknames:	The Mount Rushmore State The Coyote State
State Motto:	"Under God the People Rule"
Year of Statehood:	1889
Capital City:	Pierre
Other Major Cities:	Sioux Falls, Rapid City, Aberdeen
Population:	814,180 (2010)
Area:	77,116 square miles (199,730 square kilometers); South Dakota is the 17th largest state.
Major Industries:	farming, mining, forestry, tourism
Natural Resources:	farmland, gold, lumber
State Government:	70 representatives; 35 senators
Federal Government:	1 representative; 2 senators
Electoral Votes:	3

State Animal
coyote

State Bird
ring-necked
pheasant

Glossary

dams—barriers built across rivers to hold back water

eroded—slowly wore away

frontier—an area beyond where most people have settled

Great Plains—a region of flat or gently rolling land in the central United States; the Great Plains stretch over about one-third of the country.

gunslinger—someone who is skilled at handling and shooting a gun

immigrants—people who leave one country to live in another country

injustices—events in which a person or group is treated unfairly

Louisiana Purchase—a deal made between France and the United States; it gave the United States 828,000 square miles (2,144,510 square kilometers) of land west of the Mississippi River.

minerals—natural substances found in the earth

native—originally from a specific place

powwows—celebrations of Native American culture that often include singing and dancing

prairies—large areas of level or rolling grassland

reservations—areas of land the government has set aside for Native Americans

rodeo—an event where people compete at tasks such as bull riding and calf roping; cowboys once completed these tasks as part of their daily work.

sacred—holy or having spiritual importance

saloon—a place for eating and drinking in the Old West

service jobs—jobs that perform tasks for people or businesses

tourist—a person who travels to visit another place

traditional—relating to a custom, idea, or belief handed down from one generation to the next

treaty—an official agreement between countries, tribes, or people

To Learn More

AT THE LIBRARY

Nelson, S.D. *Black Elk's Vision: A Lakota Story.* New York, N.Y.: Abrams Books for Young Readers, 2010.

Patent, Dorothy Hinshaw. *The Horse and the Plains Indians: A Powerful Partnership.* Boston, Mass.: Clarion Books, 2012.

Yacowitz, Caryn. *South Dakota.* New York, N.Y.: Children's Press, 2009.

ON THE WEB

Learning more about South Dakota is as easy as 1, 2, 3.

1. Go to www.factsurfer.com.

2. Enter "South Dakota" into the search box.

3. Click the "Surf" button and you will see a list of related Web sites.

With factsurfer.com, finding more information is just a click away.

Index

The images in this book are reproduced through the courtesy of: Olivier, front cover (bottom); (Collection)/ Prints & Photographs Division/ Library of Congress, pp. 6, 7 (left, middle, & right); Nicholas Roemmelt/ Getty Images, pp. 8-9; Stevegeer, pp. 10-11; Tom Bean/ Alamy, p. 11 (small); Visceral Image, p. 12 (right); Serjio74, p. 12 (middle); Nate Allred, p. 12 (left); Stephen Krasemann/ Getty Images, pp. 12-13; Iofoto, pp. 14-15; Spirit of America, pp. 15 (small), 25 (small); ElsvanderGun, pp. 16-17; Harry Lands/ Alamy, p. 17 (small); Goodluz, p. 18; Kuznetcov_konstantin, p. 19 (small); Dale A. Stork, p. 20 (small); Jason Lugo/ Getty Images, pp. 20-21; RoJo Images, p. 22 (small); Justin Goode/ Getty Images, p. 23; Andre Bonn, p. 23 (small); John Warburton Lee/ SuperStock, pp. 24-25; Marek Kasula/ Alamy, p. 26 (small); Aaron Huey/ National Geographic/ SuperStock, pp. 26-27; Pakmor, p. 28 (top); UbjsP, p. 28 (bottom); Tom Reichner, p. 29 (left); Denis Pepin, p. 29 (right).

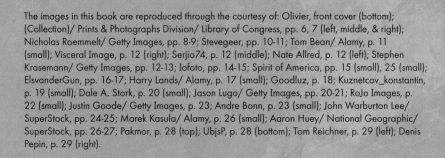